RIVETING

REPORTS

ALSO BY BRUCE ROSS-LARSON

Edit Yourself
Powerful Paragraphs
Stunning Sentences

RIVETING

REPORTS

BRUCE ROSS-LARSON

W. W. NORTON & COMPANY • NEW YORK • LONDON

The text of this book is composed in Electra
with the display set in Futura
Composition by Allentown Digital Services Division
of R. R. Donnelley & Sons Company
Manufacturing by the Haddon Craftsmen, Inc.
Book design by JAM Design

Library of Congress Cataloging-in-Publication Data

Ross-Larson, Bruce Clifford, 1942–
    Riveting reports / Bruce Ross-Larson.
        p.   cm. — (The effective writing series)
    ISBN 0-393-31793-5 (pbk.)
    1. English language—Rhetoric.   2. Report writing.   I. Title.
II. Series: Ross-Larson, Bruce Clifford, 1942–   Effective writing
series.
PE1478.R594   1999
808'.042—dc21   98-30520
                                                          CIP

W. W. Norton & Company, Inc., 500 Fifth Avenue, New York, N.Y. 10110
www.wwnorton.com

W. W. Norton & Company Ltd., 10 Coptic Street, London WC1A 1PU

*For Veruschka
and all my colleagues at the
American Writing Institute*

CONTENTS

AUTHOR'S NOTE

The techniques recommended here take the usual process of outlining, tack a few basic questions onto the front, and go beyond it into much greater detail. The idea is for you to think of your audience and your messages before you begin writing— even before you develop an outline—and to construct a paragraph-by-paragraph plan based on those messages. For if you know what your messages are and what points you're going to make, it simply is easier to write—much easier.

Having used these techniques with writing teams for fifteen years, I find that they add structure to editorial sessions and discipline to the entire process of putting together a report. The writers do, too. Of course, it is content that makes for riveting reading. The idea here is to have you separate thinking from writing (remember: to do two things at once is to do both badly) and to make sure that the process of writing doesn't get in the way of revealing your content.

I'd like to acknowledge the contributions of my colleagues at the American Writing Institute: Amy Cracknell, Andrea Brunholzl, Jessica Moore, Erika Schelble, Alison Smith, Kelli Ashley, and the interns Brendan McCarthy, Adam Calderon, Jessica Henig, and Ana Dahlman. I'd also like to acknowledge those of my editorial colleagues at Communications Development who reviewed the manuscript throughout its many stages: Meta de Coquereaumont, Alison Strong, Paul Holtz, Daphne Levitas, and Heidi Gifford. And I'd like to thank the many writers whose material I've used as examples.

BRUCE ROSS-LARSON
Washington, D.C.

RIVETING

REPORTS

AN APPROACH TO PLANNING
AND DRAFTING

MOST writers start by assembling details, examples, and comments in paragraphs—sporadically making points, rarely conveying a message. The approach here is to do the reverse—to start with your messages, to support them with points, and to use those points to assemble your details, examples, and comments.

What I suggest here is that you begin by answering a few basic questions about your topic, audience, and purpose. Next, come up with your main message and three or four supporting messages. Then use those messages to develop an outline, and move beyond that outline to formulate a detailed paragraph-by-paragraph plan for your first draft.

This may seem overly systematic, but it is just a plan, and plans change. The idea is to give your report a strong, linear foundation—and to save time when it comes to writing.

Coming up with your main and supporting messages before you start writing may seem impossible (the mere thought of it makes some writers catatonic). But what better way to structure your report than to have your messages provide your outline?

The techniques in this book are one set among many for

preparing to write. Not all people can systematically plan what they are going to write before they start drafting, and many have to start writing just to get a feel for what they're dealing with. There's no reason to deny such spontaneity. But if you're in this school, try setting your first outpouring to one side and using it as raw material for the planning and drafting techniques described here.

If you normally produce an outline before you begin writing, first try answering the six questions in Chapter 1. If you already have an outline, see how you might improve it after you've answered those questions. Then read on to see how you can open your outline into a paragraph-by-paragraph plan.

If you write from a stack of index cards covered with notes, the techniques suggested here can help you to assemble those notes. The plan you develop will help you decide which bits of your raw material fit where and which don't fit at all.

You can also use these techniques at various points in the writing process and in various situations:

- Before you write — obviously the best time to plan
- After you write — to get a sense of the structure, balance, and linearity of your argument
- If you're asking someone to write something — to have them make it perfectly explicit what they will deliver
- If you're being asked to write something — to establish a "contract" for what you will deliver and to avoid a manager's capricious changes of mind
- If you're writing with others — to avoid overlap and to have a clear idea of what your colleagues are covering in their sections or chapters

And now, the nine steps to planning and drafting your riveting report:

Step 1. Figure out what you're writing and for whom. Start by answering six simple questions. What's your main topic? Who's going to read what you write? What's your purpose in writing? How long should your report be? How much time can you spend writing? What's your working title?

Step 2. Spell out your main and supporting messages. The most important sentence in any piece of writing spells out the main message. The problem is, few writers know what their main message is, and, if they do, they either don't write it down or they bury it in the conclusion. Identifying your main message forces you to boil down everything you want to communicate about a topic into one statement. It can be descriptive or prescriptive, and you should be able to voice it easily in 25 or so words. A short piece of writing may have no supporting messages, only a series of points to support the main message. A long piece generally needs supporting messages, to make your argument clear. But avoid more than three or four if you want people to remember them.

Step 3. Use your supporting messages to develop an outline. This way your outline and headings will reinforce — and resonate with — your messages. Your main message should drive your title, and your supporting messages should drive your section headings, which generally are needed in pieces longer than a couple of pages.

Step 4. Decide how long each section will be. Given the overall page length that you've decided at the outset, assign those pages to individual sections. Because the page is merely a unit of display, try to convert those pages to numbers of paragraphs. If you're writing 10 double-spaced pages, that's around 25 paragraphs. If 15, that's around 40.

Step 5. Create a paragraph-by-paragraph plan. To each paragraph, assign the topic that you need to cover, expanding your outline of section (and possibly subsection) headings into a paragraph-by-paragraph plan. Keep in mind that this is just a start—that some paragraph topics will disappear, others will expand to two or three paragraphs.

Step 6. Make a strong point about each of your paragraph topics. To turn those topics into points, write each of them at the top of a page or screen. If you have 30 paragraph topics, you'll need 30 sheets of paper or 30 screens. Now, make a strong point about each topic in 25 to 30 words. Assembled, this clothesline of points is your full line of argument.

Step 7. Gather your details, examples, and comments. On each page, under each point, make notes to assemble your details, examples, and comments. And to make it easier to shoot down your birds of thought on the wing, spread all your pages out on a table or carry them around in a binder.

Step 8. Convert your raw material into draft paragraphs. After you've assigned all your examples, details, and other supportive material to each point, you are finally ready to begin writing. Each page of raw material can now be drafted into sentences to build a coherent paragraph. See *Powerful Paragraphs,* another volume in this series, for tips on writing paragraphs that are unified, coherent, and well developed.

Step 9. Tape your draft on a wall to apply the finishing touches. The perspective of seeing an entire draft at one glance is more illuminating than you can imagine—far more so than looking at one page at a time. With your draft taped on a wall or spread out on the floor, you can check the balance of your sections, review your line of argument, make sure your messages stand out, review your headings, and get rid of anything that doesn't fit.

So, planning means having more than a rough outline to guide your writing. It also means identifying your messages, organizing your report into sections and subsections, and arranging those sections in the most persuasive and logical order. And it means deciding the point of each paragraph—and gathering the details and examples you will call on to support each point—before you begin writing. *Drafting* thus means writing from a plan. It means making sure that your main and supporting messages are clear to your readers, and that the point of each paragraph is clear and well supported.

1

FIGURE OUT WHAT YOU'RE WRITING AND FOR WHOM

BEFORE you develop your messages and put together an outline, try to answer the following six questions—questions that writers seldom have clear answers to even after they've finished writing: What's your main topic? Who's going to read what you write? What's your purpose in writing? How long should your report be? How much time can you spend writing? What's your working title?

WHAT'S YOUR MAIN TOPIC?

Your first answer will likely be broad, so take the time to be more specific. Clearly specifying your topic narrows the boundaries of what your report will cover and keeps it from rambling or unraveling.

The first answer a team at the Census Bureau gave for a policy brief to be drawn from a massive compilation of data:

Population growth

After a bit of probing, we narrowed it to:

Projected growth of the U.S. population by state between 1995
and 2025

I immediately had a clear picture of what the policy brief would
cover.

The first answer a team at the World Bank came up with for a
chapter in the *World Development Report* on knowledge for development was just that:

Knowledge for development

Well, there are many kinds of knowledge and lots of development, past and prospective, so we narrowed the topic to:

Nurturing local and global networks of people marshaling
knowledge for human and economic development

That later changed, but at least it began to sharpen the focus.

I once had a pair of authors who wanted me to give them a
hand in putting together a book summing up three years of work
in developing a new survey method. To my deceptively simple
question, one of them answered:

A guide for policymakers on how to interpret the survey's findings

To which the other said, "No, no, no." Instead, the topic was:

A manual for statisticians on how to conduct such a survey

They went back and forth on this for about an hour, so I left.
They ended up writing two books, each on his own.

Start by writing—then refining—the first words that come into
your head. Then ask yourself the usual who? what? when?

where? how? Avoid such phrases as *a report on, a review of, an analysis of,* which can distract you from a clear statement of your topic. And test your topic on a few colleagues to see if they understand it or have something to add.

WHO'S GOING TO READ WHAT YOU WRITE?

One person or a thousand? Your supervisor or your subordinates? A small circle of experts or the public? Identifying your audience often helps you determine what you'll write and how you'll write it. It determines, in part, what sort of language to use — formal or informal, direct or diplomatic, neutral or persuasive. It also determines the length and organization of your report.

You'd be amazed at the number of times writers tell me they don't know who the audience is. Their first crack at answering is usually vague:

Policymakers

And after a bit of discussion they might identify:

Senior treasury officials responsible for international affairs

Each year the team of economists putting together the World Bank's *World Development Report* starts with something like:

Government officials

to which they add:

People in the development community more broadly

And with a bit of reflection, they add:

The press, graduate students, those in nongovernmental organizations, the public

pushing them up to 6 billion people. So we then separate their core audience:

A roundtable of key ministers in developing countries

and their secondary audiences:

Economics editors in the media, specialists in development agencies, professors and graduate students in universities

Begin by listing the people you most want to read your report from start to finish, add the people who you know will read it, then continue by adding the names of those people whose interest you would like to attract. (Don't forget to add the names of your supervisors and other reviewers.) Avoid nondescript labels, and try to identify representatives from each of your audiences. Name names, if you can. Then broaden to titles of organizations, institutions, and populations. If you are writing for more than one audience, try to distinguish your primary audience from your secondary audience.

WHAT'S YOUR PURPOSE IN WRITING?

Some reports have a clear purpose: interpreting the results of a study, introducing a new policy. Others may have lost their purpose, such as annual reports that are done the same way every year. Still others, such as fund-raising requests, mask their purpose intentionally.

For that Census Bureau policy brief I mentioned earlier, the first statement of purpose was:

To inform the public about U.S. census projections

After considerable pushing, we narrowed it:

To persuade state and local governments that the population projections provide a sound basis for planning

It's easy to inform. It's not easy to persuade. And almost all reports are meant to persuade someone of something.

For a policy report by the Benton Foundation and Libraries for the Future, the first attempt at the purpose was:

To show the importance of libraries in the digital age

That was quickly refined to this:

To persuade librarians, policymakers, foundations, and corporations of the importance of libraries as resource centers for the new communications and information tools in this digital age

Compare the timid *show the importance of* with the stronger *persuade*, surrounded by concrete detail.

So, to say that you are writing to *inform* your audience about your topic is not enough: there is almost always another purpose.

The following verbs all avoid the specific:

communicate
emphasize
describe
explore
tell
consider
suggest

while these verbs can push you toward greater detail and clarity:

create
persuade
promote
take
convince
force
motivate
quell
change
push

If you're having trouble identifying your purpose, ask yourself: What do you want your audience to do after reading your report? Adopt your recommendations? Formulate a new set of policies? Change their behavior? Sometimes your purpose may have a hidden agenda—to get a promotion or change the way your department is organized.

HOW LONG SHOULD YOUR REPORT BE?

Or better still: How much time will your audience devote to reading it? If only 10 minutes, your report should be about 10 double-spaced pages. It may be hard to chop 90 pages off your planned 100-pager, but remember that few people read an entire report, no matter how riveting, and that shorter reports are usually tighter—and better written.

Many people come up with an imprecise estimate:

However long it ends up

or:

Around 10 to 20 pages

Much more useful is:

10 double-spaced pages of typescript

On average, your readers cruise along at about 250 words a minute, or roughly 1 double-spaced page a minute. So if your audience is spending 10 minutes on your report, that's 2,500 words, or 10 double-spaced pages.

That's precisely what we came up with for a report on urban poverty for the Rockefeller Foundation. Millions of dollars in research. Thousands of pages of write-ups. Twelve researchers and project managers sitting around a conference table, thinking, no doubt, that their policy report would run 100 to 200 pages. But the discipline of tailoring the length of the report to the attention that it might command from legislators and senior administration officials led us to 10 double-spaced pages.

Once you have an estimate of the number of pages (units of display), try to convert that into numbers of paragraphs (units of composition). If you're writing 10 double-spaced pages, that's roughly 25 paragraphs (at 2.5 per page). And if you're writing 10 single-spaced pages, that's roughly 40 paragraphs (at 4 per page).

If the length of your report gets out of hand, prepare an executive summary. And if the summary gets too long for your core audience, try a cover note that presents your messages.

HOW MUCH TIME CAN YOU SPEND WRITING?

Writing, at least the writing of reports, is usually preceded by the separate processes of research and analysis. Keep that in mind when estimating the amount of time you will spend on a report. Also keep in mind that other things are sure to intrude on your time.

Here, too, people are imprecise:

As long as it takes

Compare that with:

First draft: 5 days, 8 hours a day, to be finished May 1.
Revised final draft: 3 days, 4 hours a day, to be finished May 15.

Give your estimate in clock time rather than calendar days, and think about multiplying that estimate by 2 or 3 to account for optimism and unexpected interruptions.

Because most people squeeze writing in at the end of the research-analysis-writing cycle, try to begin planning before you start writing, during the analysis and even the research, and include time for review and revision.

WHAT'S YOUR WORKING TITLE?

The title is your first chance to engage your reader, so be brief, honest, and communicative.

Compare this first attempt:

African Import Prices: 1970, 1980, and 1990

with this final:

Do African Countries Pay More for Their Exports? Yes

Imports?   ?

The title made the difference for a World Bank working paper, reviewed by every major African newspaper as well as London's *Financial Times.*

Another conventional title:

Strategies for Implementing Reform

injected with a bit of urgency:

Reform Can't Wait

And a typically bureaucratic title:

Economic Growth and Public Investment

made a bit more engaging:

From Boom to Bust—and Back?

The overview of a recent *Human Development Report* had this as the title of its opening chapter:

Overview

But it was the following title that put the overview on the map:

The Revolution for Gender Equality

Here's another title that may have been true:

A Comparative Analysis of Commodity-Dependent Economies in Developing Countries but that became the subtitle for the more memorable:

Plundering Agriculture

The best titles are memorable and easy to repeat. A *Comparative Analysis of Commodity-Dependent Economies in Developing Countries* did not fall trippingly off the tongue, but *Plundering Agriculture* remains in readers' minds years after publication.

In your titles, avoid words like:

procedures for
overview of
experiment in
review of
findings of
summary of
report on
issues surrounding
strategy for
implications of
investigation into

And don't get stuck with your first working title, as most writers do. Instead, continually scrutinize your working title to see how you can further refine it to be true to your messages and readers.

2

SPELL OUT YOUR MAIN AND SUPPORTING MESSAGES

FEW writers think of the messages they are trying to communicate in a report. That is why I also try to spell out the main message in 25 to 30 words and three or four supporting messages, each of them in 25 to 30 words. The idea is to build a hierarchy: main message → supporting messages → points (one to a paragraph) → details, examples, and comments. Most writers wallow in the details, occasionally making a point, rarely voicing a message.

One reason they wallow is that it's not easy to spell out messages. I once spent six hours with a high-powered team at the Federal Reserve Board trying to come up with the message structure for a five-year strategic plan. The team thought that four sentences in six hours was wildly unproductive, but they had much more: agreement by all of them for the first time on what the plan should cover.

In coming up with your messages, will you move from the general to the specific? Will you divide a problem into its parts or provide solutions to a problem? Will you describe a process? (For more on shaping your argument, see Chapter 3.) And as you temporize with supporting messages, decide how to arrange them. You should also check to be sure that one of your supporting messages isn't really your main message.

YOUR MAIN MESSAGE

The most important question about any piece of writing is: *What is the main message you want to convey?* The main message is the single most important idea that you want your reader to walk away with. Answering this question forces you to boil down into one statement everything you know about your topic and everything you hope to achieve by writing about it. If *you* don't articulate it, your reader certainly won't be able to.

As with the title, the main message will help you decide what to keep and what to cut by defining the boundaries of your report. Also like the title, the main message should do more than describe or inform — it should compel. Don't leave your readers in suspense. Remember, they may not have much time to read your report. Use simple language, and load value into your main message. Also remember that supporting messages follow, so don't overload it.

Messages classify and describe things (descriptive messages) or recommend action (prescriptive messages).

Some first attempts at a main message are too general:

New technology can have a beneficial effect on communities.

so think about adding a bit of detail:

New communications technologies can strengthen neighborhoods, create new opportunities for participation in civic affairs, and promote economic development on a scale that enhances, rather than undermines, life in communities.

Some attempts at coming up with the main message leave the reader with a *So what?*

Economic policies are often dominated by political considerations.

This can often be fixed by adding a *Because* to the front of the first statement and continuing with the action recommended:

Because economic policies are often dominated by political considerations, economists must maintain contact with their roots and be more willing to accept innovation and change.

What do you really want to say? Keep the answer short and simple—you should be able to voice it easily. And try reading your main message aloud to colleagues to see if they can repeat it back to you. If they can't, the message may be too long (more than 30 words?), too vague, or too complicated.

YOUR SUPPORTING MESSAGES

A short piece of writing may not have supporting messages, relying instead on a series of points to support the main message. A longer piece generally needs supporting messages, but you should avoid having more than three or four if you want your readers to remember them. Your supporting messages divide your argument and thus become the conceptual architecture that informs your outline.

Here's the main message for that Rockefeller Foundation report I mentioned in Chapter 1:

Higher program participation, higher placement in jobs, higher pay—these are the payoffs possible from an integrated program of education and employment that can be delivered at reasonable cost.

And here are the supporting messages:

Job training should develop specific work skills.

Basic skills training should be related to the job.

Education and employment programs should be tied to the requirements of industry.

Those programs should also be tailored to the individual.

Training should be surrounded with a full array of support services.

These five sentences are the essence of what the research team wanted to communicate to legislators and program administrators. It took 12 people half a day to come up with them.

Here, the main message for the *World Development Report 1997:*

An effective, capable state is vital for the provision of the goods and services, rules, and institutions that allow markets to flourish and people to lead healthier, happier lives.

And here, the supporting messages:

To make the state a more effective partner in a country's development, the state's role should be matched to its capability.

Raising a state's capability so that it reinvigorates public institutions means first designing effective rules and restraints that check arbitrary state actions and combat entrenched corruption.

Removing obstacles to state reform will only succeed if efforts are directed by leaders with a clear vision of the way things could be, and a contagious determination to turn that vision into reality.

In a World Bank report for governments and the media in the Middle East and North Africa, the main message set the challenge echoed in the report's title, *Claiming the Future:*

By 2010 the countries of the Middle East and North Africa have the potential to double incomes, increase life expectancy by close to 10 years, and cut illiteracy and infant mortality by almost half.

And the supporting messages elaborated on the promise:

They could become full partners in the global economy using integration with Europe and within the region as a stepping stone to international competitiveness.

The faster economic growth would reduce poverty and bring down unemployment, restoring hope to millions.

Peace, macroeconomic stability, and an attractive investment environment could attract billions of dollars of capital from nationals and foreign investors.

In a chapter in a recent *Human Development Report* entitled "Still an Unequal World," the main message was

In no society today do women enjoy the same opportunities as men.

And the supporting messages:

This unequal status leaves considerable disparities between how much women contribute to human development and how little they share in its benefits.

A widespread pattern of inequality between women and men persists—in their access to education, health and nutrition, and even more in their participation in the economic and political spheres.

Women now share much more in the benefits of social services, both public and private—but continue to be denied equal opportunities for political and economic participation.

Women do not enjoy the same protection and rights as men in the laws of many countries.

Announced in the opening paragraph of that chapter, these messages drove the headings for the content that followed.

Here's the main message for a short policy brief on population projections from the Census Bureau:

As the U.S. population rises by 72 million over the next 30 years—to 335 million in 2025—more of us will live in the South and West, be elderly, and have Hispanic and Asian roots.

And the supporting messages, with their numerical detail:

The South and West will add 59 million residents by 2025— 82 percent of the projected growth to 2025—with more than

30 million people in just three states: California, Texas, and Florida.

Also by 2025, the population 65 and older will rise by 28 million people—39 percent of the projected growth—and bring to 27 the number of states where a fifth of their people will be elderly. Only Florida is close today.

The Hispanic and Asian populations will together gain 44 million people and constitute 24 percent of the total population in 2025, up from 14 percent today. California, Texas, and Florida will gain 20 million Hispanics.

Again, these four sentences were strung together—with bullets—to open the brief and, as you'll see in the next chapters, drive the headings for the content that followed.

3

USE YOUR SUPPORTING MESSAGES TO DEVELOP AN OUTLINE

THERE are many ways to break up your topic. For a short piece, look at your main message and see whether the topic lends itself to orderly division. For a long piece, try to discern the relations among the supporting messages to come up with your section headings. Will you move from the general to the particular? Will you divide a problem into its parts? Will you consider different things at different times? Will you group things or separate them? Your section headings should reflect your treatment of the topic.

Subsections are broken up in the same way as sections. If you have two or three sections and the piece is 15 to 20 pages long, you might want as many as four or five subsections in each section. But if you have many sections, you should have only a few subsections, if any, in each.

Your outline and, thus, your architecture will vary with your material, your audience, your constraints. The common structure of the typical academic research paper is *background, method, findings, implications,* and *conclusions,* headings that communicate no content. Compare those headings with *Rethinking the state—the world over,* which is beginning to communicate content. If you must use preordained section headings, try getting creative with your subsection headings, letting your messages drive them rather than the section headings. And if that's not possible, try writing an executive summary with headings driven by your message structure.

These messages:

As the U.S. population rises by 72 million over the next 30 years—to 335 million in 2025—more of us will live in the South and West, be elderly, and have Hispanic and Asian roots.

The South and West will add 59 million residents by 2025— 82 percent of the projected growth to 2025—with more than 30 million people in just three states: California, Texas, and Florida.

Also by 2025, the population 65 and older will rise by 28 million people—39 percent of the projected growth—and bring to 27 the number of states where a fifth of their people will be elderly. Only Florida is close today.

The Hispanic and Asian populations will together gain 44 million people and constitute 24 percent of the total population in 2025, up from 14 percent today. California, Texas, and Florida will have 20 million Hispanics.

became the pillars of this outline:

Americans Are Getting Older, Warmer, More Diverse
Opening (no section heading)
  1. Different paths to growth
  2. 27 Floridas
  3. Big gains for Hispanics and Asians

Note how this outline (and eventual table of contents) communicates the essence of the report's content to readers:

Claiming the Future—Choosing Prosperity in the Middle East and North Africa

1. Disengagement from the changing global economy
   a. Missing out on globalization
   b. Domestic policies are ill suited to new global realities
2. Yesterday's achievements, today's predicament
   a. Achievements of the statist era were considerable
   b. Past successes were the outcome of easier times, not statist policies
   c. Why change has been slow
3. The promise of prosperity
   a. Some aspects of the international environment are favorable
   b. Many of the conditions in the Middle East and North Africa are favorable
   c. Jordan, Morocco, and Tunisia are beginning to reap the rewards of reform
4. From politics to economics
   a. Now is the time for action
   b. Choosing to be prosperous
   c. Politics in the service of economics

As does this:

The State in a Changing World

1. Rethinking the state—the world over
   a. The evolving role of the state
   b. Refocusing on the effectiveness of the state
2. Matching role to capability
   a. Securing the economic and social fundamentals
   b. Fostering markets: liberalization, regulation, and industrial policy
3. Reinvigorating institutional capability
   a. Building institutions for a capable public sector

4

DECIDE HOW LONG EACH SECTION WILL BE

AFTER you have developed an outline, decide how many paragraphs you will have in each section and subsection. Start with the number of pages you feel appropriate for the entire piece. Because double-spaced typescript usually has 2 to 3 paragraphs per page and single-spaced 4 to 5, multiply the number of pages by 2.5 for double-spaced typescript or 4 for single-spaced, the average number of paragraphs per page. The reason for doing this is that pages are merely units of display, while paragraphs are units of composition.

For the Census Bureau's policy brief on population projections to 2025, we came up with a maximum of 6 double-spaced pages and assigned them thus:

Americans Are Getting Older, Warmer, More Diverse

	No. double-spaced pages	No. paragraphs
Total	6	16
(Opening—no heading)	1	2
Different paths to growth	2	5
27 Floridas	1	3
Big gains for Hispanics and Asians	2	6

For the overview of the recent *World Development Report* on the state in a changing world, the estimated length was 30 pages. That meant about 75 paragraphs (2.5 × 30), which were assigned to the various sections and subsections in this way:

The Future of the State

	No. double-spaced pages	No. paragraphs
Total	30	75
Opening	2	5
Rethinking the state—the world over	2	5
A two-part strategy	2	3
Matching role to capability	7	16
The first job of states: getting the fundamentals right		7
Going beyond the basics: the state need not be the sole provider		6
Knowing the states limits		3
Reinvigorating state institutions	10	25
Effective rules and restraints		4
Subjecting the state to more competition		9
Bringing the state closer to people		9
Strategic options for reform		3
Beyond national borders: facilitating global action	3	10
Collective action		5
Embracing external competition		3
Promoting global collective action		2
Removing obstacles to state reform	4	11

5

CREATE A PARAGRAPH-BY-PARAGRAPH PLAN

YOU now know roughly the number of paragraphs you will have in each section. The next step is to assign a topic to each of those paragraphs. What you will end up with is a list of paragraph topics in the order they will appear in your report, interspersed among your section and subsection headings—in short, a paragraph-by-paragraph plan of places to gather your material. Don't worry about getting the list of paragraph topics right the first time. The first list will suggest other topics in different order. And as you begin to write, many of the topics will be divided or collapsed. But the more time you spend on this, the more solid the structure of your argument.

Paragraph-by-paragraph plans can be made at any stage of the writing process. I often prepare one for manuscripts that I edit—to get me quickly up to speed on content, structure, and balance. But it is most helpful to make one in the planning stage, after you've determined your messages and section headings, and then revise it when you have completed your first draft. The revised one will help you stay aware of changes in structure and the continuing relevance of your messages. Showing your paragraph plan to the people who will be reviewing your report—or to your fellow authors in a group project—is a good way to have them buy into what you're planning write. It also allows them to comment before you've invested a lot of time in writing.

Here is the paragraph-by-paragraph plan for the Census Bureau's policy brief:

Introduction (no heading)
¶1. Summary of messages
¶2. Quotation from analyst Paul Campbell: "Keep in mind that these are just projections . . ."

Different paths to growth
¶3. California, Texas, and Florida take different paths
¶4. California's losses through interstate migration
¶5. Texas's gains from all three contributors
¶6. Florida's small natural increase
¶7. Biggest interstate migration—New York

27 Floridas
¶8. 27 states will have one in five people elderly
¶9. 21 states will double their 65 and older population
¶10. Youth population—Alaska will have largest gains

Big gains for Hispanics and Asians
¶11. Hispanics and Asians and Pacific Islanders—61 percent of the growth
¶12. Big gains in California and the East
¶13. Growth in Black population in Georgia, Texas, Florida, Maryland, and Virginia
¶14. Growth in White population in Florida, Texas, Washington, North Carolina, and Georgia
¶15. Native American population rising
¶16. Campbell quotation: "What might seem unusual today will be usual tomorrow . . ."

6

MAKE A STRONG POINT ABOUT EACH OF YOUR PARAGRAPH TOPICS

WRITE the first topic of your paragraph-by-paragraph plan at the top of a sheet of paper (or at the top of a fresh page on your word processor), and make a strong point about it. If you have a general topic such as this:

Topic Partnerships of governments, businesses, and citizens

you might move to a strong point such as this:

Point When governments listen to businesses and citizens and work in partnership with them in deciding and implementing policy, they create programs that people will support.

Now do the same for all the other topics in your plan. You'll find for some that it's easy, and for others, impossible—and that will suggest refinements to your plan.

Here are some examples of moving from topic to point for the Census Bureau's brief on projections:

Topic California, Texas, and Florida take different paths

↓

Point California, Texas, and Florida will probably see the
most growth but they will grow in very different ways.

Topic California's losses through interstate migration

↓

Point California will see big gains through natural increase
and international migration but big losses through interstate migration.

Topic Texas's gains from all three contributors

↓

Point In Texas there will be a balance among all three contributors to its rising population.

Here's a set of topic-to-point conversions for the overview of
the recent *World Development Report*:

Topic New ideas about the role of the state

↓

Point The world is changing and with it our ideas about the
state's role in economic and social development.

Topic Expectations met, but not everywhere

↓

Point In a few countries things have indeed worked out more
or less as the technocrats expected, but in many countries outcomes were very different.

Topic Government getting bigger

↓

Point Over the last century the size and scope of government have expanded enormously, particularly in the industrial countries.

Topic Focus on state inspired by dramatic events

↓

Point As in the 1940s, today's renewed focus on the state's role has been inspired by dramatic events in the global economy, which have fundamentally changed the environment in which states operate.

Topic Clamor for more effective governance

↓

Point The clamor for greater government effectiveness has reached crisis proportions in many developing countries where the state has failed to deliver even such fundamental public goods as roads, property rights, and basic health and education.

7

GATHER YOUR DETAILS, EXAMPLES, AND COMMENTS

ON each page, under each point—20 for a 20-paragraph report, 100 for a 100-paragraph report—begin noting your support—data, details, examples, and comments. It helps to spread all your pages out on a large table. I generally carry them around in a binder. That allows jotting down—and not losing—ideas that come to mind. It also allows working on one paragraph at a time.

The support for some of your points will fill some pages quickly, while others remain empty. If one point is short on detail and examples, you may need to compile more information by doing more research. If you can't support a point well, consider cutting it. And remember, an ounce of example is worth a ton of abstract generalization.

Here are examples from the Rockefeller Foundation's report:

Point   The integrated model provides in-depth training in the skills required for a specific job and—just as important—places heavy emphasis on work habits.

Support Less intensive programs offer little to those with special disadvantages

- Development of life skills
- Stresses punctuality and attendance

Point   The integrated model provides literacy and numeracy training concurrently with job training.

Support Only elements directly related to job included
- Just-in-time remediation of basic skills speeds learning process
- The closer the tie between job skills and basic literacy and numeracy training, the more willing trainees are to increase basic skills

Point   Another key feature of the integrated model is to have the education and employment program plugged directly into the requirements of industry — and to have industry plugged into the development of the program.

Support When the demand and wages for a skill fall, it is phased out of the skill offerings
- Technical instructors drawn from industry
- Approach treats training as a business

Having all your material slotted into a paragraph-by-paragraph plan enables you to refine it *before* you've written a paragraph.

8

CONVERT YOUR RAW MATERIAL INTO DRAFT PARAGRAPHS

WITH the contents of each paragraph roughed out, the material of your paragraphs is now before you. Writing the perfect paragraph still won't be easy, but it should be much easier now that you have planned the order and content of each one.

Rough out your paragraphs by numbering your supporting elements—details, examples, and comments—in the order they might appear. Details that complement each other might be combined into one sentence. Paragraphs that are long and bristling with numbers may work better as a table or chart. Be especially careful to put dates or statistics in a logical order. Strike out unnecessary detail, and move elsewhere material that is not relevant to your point.

California will see big gains through natural increase and international migration but big losses through interstate migration.

- Projected increase of 17.7 million residents in the next 30 years
- California is the most populous state
- One in eight Americans live in California

- One in seven Americans will live in California by 2025
- The largest natural increase
- The largest net international migration
- The second largest inflow of interstate migrants
- The largest outflow of interstate migrants

The paragraph:

> With California's projected increase of 17.7 million residents in the next 30 years, one American in seven will live in California by 2025, up from one in eight today. For this most populous of states, everything happens in a big way: the largest natural increase, the largest net international migration, the second largest inflow of interstate migrants, and the largest outflow of interstate migrants.

A solid first draft.

The following sections contain a few paragraph models (drawn from the companion book *Powerful Paragraphs*) to help you convert your raw material into draft paragraphs.

LEAD WITH THE POINT AND SUPPORT IT

The most common way to develop a paragraph is to state the point in the first sentence and support it, in subsequent sentences, with evidence: details, examples, and comments. When you lead with the point, your reader can identify it immediately, and a skimmer can pick up your line of argument by reading the first sentence of each paragraph. This form of development is what most of us use for two-thirds of our writing. It becomes less effective when overused, and more when alternated with other ways of developing a point.

> *Over the past century, the human race has been affected by a slew of what demographers call "secular" trends. One such*

trend is an increase in average size. You have to stoop to get through the doorways of a Tudor cottage in England because its inhabitants were smaller than you are, not because they had a penchant for crouching. Another trend is in life expectancy. People are living longer. Life expectancy in Africa increased over the past 20 years from 46 to 53 years. Over the same period in Europe, where things were already pretty comfortable to begin with, life expectancy increased from 71 to 75 years. The global average was an increase from 58 to 65 years.

LEAD WITH THE POINT AND CONCLUDE WITH A COMMENT

Concluding a paragraph with a comment can inject a bit of your personality and, at times, humor. A comment can also put a paragraph in perspective, create a bridge to the next paragraph, or reinforce your point after presenting a series of facts.

Geography is not geology, but they can be interlinked in surprising ways. Geographically, Sakhalin Island is part of the Russian Far East, though half of it was Japanese territory until 1945. Geographically, though, it is a northward extension of Japan and thus prone to the same sort of seismic ups and downs as the rest of that archipelago. Earthquakes are no respectors of political boundaries.

LEAD WITH THE POINT AND FOLLOW IT WITH A BULLETED LIST

A list of numerical facts, complicated details, or recommendations can be difficult for readers to lift off the page from a block of text. Breaking that block into bulleted items clarifies those elements, a style good for setting up a line of argument.

The ratio of global trade to GDP has been rising over the past decade, but it has been falling for 44 developing countries, with more than a billion people. *The least developed countries, with 10% of the world's people, have only 0.3% of world trade* — half their share of two decades ago.

The list goes on:

- More than half of all developing countries have been bypassed by foreign direct investment, two-thirds of which has gone to only eight developing countries.
- Real commodity prices in the 1990s were 45% lower than those in the 1980s — and 10% lower than the lowest level during the Great Depression, reached in 1932.
- The terms of trade for the least developed countries have declined a cumulative 50% over the past 25 years.
- Average tariffs on industry country imports from the least developed countries are 30% higher than the global average.
- Developing countries lose about $60 billion a year from agricultural subsidies and barriers to textile exports in industrial nations.

CONCLUDE WITH THE POINT AFTER INTRODUCING THE SUBJECT

Occasionally, put the point at the end of a paragraph to build suspense. One way to conclude with the point: introduce a subject, discuss it, then make a point about it at the end.

Imagine that a mad scientist went back to 1950 and offered to transport the median family to the wondrous world of the 1990s, and to place them at, say, the 25th percentile level. The 25th percentile of 1996 is a clear material improvement over the median of 1950. Would they accept his offer? Almost surely not—because in 1950 they were middle class, while in 1996 they would be poor, even if they lived better in material terms. *People don't just care about their absolute material level, they care about their level compared with others.*

START WITH A QUESTION AND ANSWER IT IMMEDIATELY

Asking a question in the first line of a paragraph grabs readers' attention and sets up your point. Using an immediate, direct answer to make your point demonstrates a firm stance, emphasized by the surety of a fragment.

So will squash eventually rival tennis as a spectator sport, and will Jansher Khan and Peter Marshall become as rich and famous as Pete Sampras and Andre Agassi? *Almost certainly not.* For all the gimmicks of a glasswalled court, a special white ball and more and better cameras, squash remains fearsomely difficult to televise. Not only does the ball move too fast but the camera lens foreshortens the action. Squash, therefore, is destined to remain a sport better played than watched. Given its propensity for what the tennis authorities term "audible obscenities", that may be just as well.

9

TAPE YOUR DRAFT ON A WALL TO APPLY THE FINISHING TOUCHES

A little-used but wildly effective technique is taping your entire draft report on a wall. That permits many things. One is to see more than a page at a time—indeed, to see all the pages at a time. Only by so doing can you assess overall structure and the balance of your sections and subsections. This also makes it easier to track your various levels of headings, switching sections to subsections and vice versa. And it makes it easier to revise your headings, injecting more punch, ensuring parallel treatment as appropriate.

A second virtue of taping your draft on a wall is that it puts the writer and reviewer side by side, dealing with the problems of a draft, rather than face to face, in the usually uncomfortable confrontation.

A third is that it allows you to make cuts quickly. If you need to cut a 50-page draft to 20 or 30 pages, it's the best technique. I use it for slash-and-burn editing, especially *stripping*—crossing out most sentences in a succession of paragraphs—lifting the points, and then stringing the points together to form new paragraphs.

REVIEW YOUR LINE OF ARGUMENT

To distinguish the levels of your headings, use a marker to circle all your A-level section headings and underline all your B-level subsection headings. Are there blocks of argument that would work better elsewhere? Look first at your sections, seeing whether you should move any of them. Next look at your subsections— and then at your paragraphs. Ask yourself whether your ideas flow in a logical and obvious way. If not, you may want to change some of your section and subsection headings to make the progression of your argument clearer.

SPOTLIGHT YOUR MESSAGES

The messages of a report or chapter are too often buried in the last 3 or 4 pages. Move them up front so that readers don't have to wait for them. Your readers should know your main message after reading only the first few paragraphs.

ADJUST LENGTH AND BALANCE

Think again about your target audience. How much do your readers really want, or need, to read? Look for duplication of information across sections, for long explanations of concepts that your readers may already know, and for tangents that sidetrack your argument. If you have a highly detailed or technical section, consider making it an appendix at the end of your report. If you cut or combine sections, you may need to adjust the balance of your report. Try to keep the sections roughly similar in length.

REFINE YOUR TITLE AND SECTION HEADINGS

You've been continually revising your title, now give it another test. Does it convey your message? For the example here, we moved from this title:

Growing the Economies of the Middle East and North Africa

to:

Claiming the Future: Choosing Prosperity in the Middle East and North Africa

After the title, take a look at headings. How could they better convey your messages? Headings engage your reader, so don't leave them empty.

A two-hour wall session with the lead authors of a World Bank policy research report on aid effectiveness began with this outline of headings:

Rethinking Aid
The new international environment
New thinking on development strategy
Aid and development
Aid, policy reform, and conditionality
Aid and public expenditures
Aid and the institutions for public services
Rethinking development agencies

Those became:

Assessing Aid: What Works, What Doesn't, and Why
New thinking on development strategy
Money matters in a good policy environment

Aid as the midwife of good policies
Money matters—in a good institutional environment
Aid as the midwife of good institutions
Moving aid from money to ideas

Far more informative.

TAKE A LAST LOOK

Before ripping your report off the wall, make sure that any changes you made in the last few sections didn't displace another element. Now you are ready to edit line by line to make your report absolutely riveting. (See *Powerful Paragraphs, Stunning Sentences,* also in this series, and *Edit Yourself.*) Last, do a spell-check and final leaf-through to pick up incidental flaws that might unnecessarily distract your readers.

EXEMPLARY REPORTS: FROM START TO FINISH

From a policy brief for the U.S. Census Bureau

TOPIC, AUDIENCE, AND PURPOSE

What's the main topic?

State-by-state population changes to 2025

Who's going to read what you write?

Regular Census Brief distribution list of several thousand journalists, businesspeople, academics, and commerce colleagues

What's your purpose in writing?

To spotlight the marginal changes in population by region, by age group, by race/ethnic group—with state stories where interesting

How long should your report be?

6 double-spaced pages, or 15 paragraphs

How much time can you spend writing?

> Draft plan: 1/2 day (deadline: September 15)
> Draft brief: 5 days, 8 hours a day (deadline: September 28)
> (Printing in early October)

What's your working title?

> Americans Are Getting Warmer, Older, More Diverse

MESSAGES

What is the message you want to convey?

> As the U.S. population rises by 72 million over the next 30 years—to 335 million in 2025—more of us will live in the South and West, be elderly, and have Hispanic and Asian roots.

What are the supporting messages?

- The South and West will add 59 million residents by 2025—82 percent of the projected growth to 2025—with more than 30 million people in just three states: California, Texas, and Florida.
- Also by 2025, the population 65 and older will rise by 28 million people—39 percent of the projected growth—and bring to 27 the number of states where a fifth of their people will be elderly. Only Florida is close today.
- The Hispanic and Asian populations will together gain 44 million people and constitute 24 percent of the total population in 2025, up from 14 percent today. California, Texas, and Florida will gain 20 million Hispanics.

OUTLINE HEADINGS

Americans Are Getting Older, Warmer, More Diverse

	No. double-spaced pages	No. paragraphs
Total	6	16
Sections		
(Opening—no heading)	1	2
Different paths to growth	2	5
27 Floridas	1	3
Big gains for Hispanics and Asians	2	6

PARAGRAPH PLAN

Introduction (no heading)
¶1. Older, warmer, more diverse
¶2. Quotation from analyst Paul Campbell: "Keep in mind that these are just projections . . ."

Different paths to growth
¶3. California, Texas, and Florida take different paths
¶4. California's losses through interstate migration
¶5. Texas's gains from all three contributors
¶6. Florida's small natural increase
¶7. Biggest interstate migration—New York

27 Floridas
¶8. 27 states will have one in five people elderly
¶9. 21 states will double their 65 and older population
¶10. Youth population—Alaska will have largest gains

Big gains for Hispanics and Asians
¶11. Hispanics and Asians and Pacific Islanders—61 percent of the growth

¶12. Big gains in California and the East

¶13. Growth in Black population in Georgia, Texas, Florida, Maryland, and Virginia

¶14. Growth in White population in Florida, Texas, Washington, North Carolina, and Georgia

¶15. American Indian population rising

¶16. Campbell quotation: "What might seem unusual today will be usual tomorrow . . ."

SAMPLE PARAGRAPH CONTENTS

Paragraph topic:

California's losses through interstate migration

Make a strong point about the topic:

California will see big gains through natural increase and international migration but big losses through interstate migration.

List your supporting details, examples, and comments:

- Projected increase of 17.7 millions residents in the next 30 years
- California is the most populous state
- One in eight Americans lives in California
- One in seven will live in California by 2025
- The largest natural increase
- The largest net international migration
- The second largest inflow of interstate migrants
- The largest outflow of interstate migrants

Paragraph draft:

California's losses through interstate migration. With its projected increase of 17.7 million residents in the next 30 years, one American in seven will live in California by 2025, up from one in eight today. For this most populous of states, everything happens in a big way: the largest natural increase, the largest net international migration, the second largest inflow of interstate migrants, and the largest outflow of interstate migrants.

FIRST DRAFT

Getting Warmer, Older, More Diverse: *State-by-State Population Changes to 2025*

As the U.S. population rises by 72 million over the next 30 years—to 335 million in 2025—more of us will live in the South and West, be elderly, and have Hispanic and Asian roots.

- The South and West will add 59 million residents by 2025—82 percent of the projected growth to 2025—with more than 30 million people in just three states: California, Texas, and Florida.
- Also by 2025, the population 65 and older will rise by 28 million people—39 percent of the projected growth—and bring to 27 the number of states where a fifth of their people will be elderly. Only Florida is close today.
- The Hispanic and Asian populations will together gain 44 million people and constitute 24 percent of the total population in 2025, up from 14 percent today. California, Texas, and Florida will gain 20 million Hispanics.

Putting these numbers in perspective, Census Bureau analyst Paul Campbell said, "Keep in mind that these are just projections. I don't think we're wrong about the big trends, such as regional growth or the growth in the population 65 and older. But the projections do not drive reality. They come from projecting past trends into the future, and those trends can change—especially international migration, state-to-state movements, even births and deaths."

Different paths to growth

California, Texas, and Florida are expected to account for 45 percent of the nation's population growth from 1995 to 2025. But the main contributors to rising population—natural increase, interstate migration, and international migration—operate very differently in the three states.

California's losses through interstate migration. With its projected increase of 17.7 million residents in the next 30 years, one American in seven will live in California by 2025, up from one in eight today. For this most populous of states, everything happens in a big way: the largest natural increase, the largest net international migration, the second largest inflow of interstate migrants, and the largest outflow of interstate migrants.

Texas's gains from all three contributors. Distinguishing Texas's increase of 8.5 million is the balance among all three contributors to its rising population—with a large natural increase, high net interstate migration, and significant net international migration.

Florida's small natural increase. For Florida's increase of 6.5 million people from 1995 to 2025, the natural increase is low because of its already gray population. But it has the highest net interstate migration along with substantial net international migration.

The biggest interstate migration story is New York, which loses 13.1 million residents to other states and attracts only 8.0 million new residents, for a net loss of 5.1 million. By 2020 Florida will replace New York as the third most populous state.

27 Floridas

With baby boomers beginning to hit retirement age in 2010, 27 states will have one in five people elderly in 2025. And every state but Alaska and California will have 15 percent or more of their population 65 and older in 2025, up from a mere four states in 1995.

Twenty-one states will at least double their 65 and older population. Except for New Hampshire, all these states are in the South or West.

What about the other end of the age structure? Alaska will have the greatest proportion of its population under 20 years of age in 2025, followed by California, Utah, Texas, and New Mexico.

Big gains for Hispanics and Asians

Hispanics and Asians and Pacific Islanders, with 14 percent of today's population, will drive 61 percent of the growth—44 percent from Hispanics and 17 percent from Asians.

California will add 12 million Hispanics to its population while Texas and Florida combined will add 8 million Hispanics. Forty-one percent of the nation's Asian population will live in California, with a jump from 3.6 million in 1995 to 9.1 million in 2025. But there will also be big gains in the East for Asians, with New York and New Jersey adding a combined 3.0 (or 1.6) million by 2025.

Florida and Texas are each expected to add about 1.9 million Blacks to their populations—and along with California, they will surpass New York as the states with the largest Black population. Most of the growth for Blacks will be in Georgia, Texas, Florida, Maryland, and Virginia.

And most of that for Whites will be in Florida, Texas, Washington, North Carolina, and Georgia.

The American Indian population is set to rise by nearly half, with the biggest gains in New Mexico, Oklahoma, and

Arizona. In 2025, about 46 percent of American Indians will reside in just five states—Oklahoma, Arizona, New Mexico, California, and Washington.

As Campbell concluded, "What might seem unusual today will be usual tomorrow, as our population continues to grow older, more diverse, more interested in living in the South and West."

EXEMPLARY REPORTS: FROM PLAN TO DRAFT

From the overview to the World Development Report 1997

HERE'S a look at the hierarchy of drafting, moving from topic → point → raw material → draft paragraph:

Topic New ideas about the role of the state

↓

Point The world is changing and with it our ideas about the state's role in economic and social development.

↓

Support

- Focus on state today similar to past
- Changing role brought about by dramatic events
- State saw itself as leader for change, too simplistic
- Development was viewed as a largely technical challenge
- Flexibility valued over checks and balances

↓

Draft

The world is changing and with it our ideas about the state's role in economic and social development. Today's intense focus on the state's role is reminiscent of an earlier era, when the world was emerging from the ravages of World War II, and much of the developing world was just gaining its independence. Then development seemed a more easily surmountable—and largely technical—challenge. State-led intervention emphasized market failures and accorded the state a central role in correcting them. But this worldview, as we all realize today, was too simplistic. Flexibility to implement policies devised by technocrats was accorded pride of place. Accountability through checks and balances was regarded as an encumbrance.

Topic Expectations met, but not everywhere

↓

Point In a few countries things have indeed worked out more or less as the technocrats expected, but in many countries outcomes were very different.

↓

Support

- Government schemes
- Private investors held back
- Rulers acted arbitrarily
- Corruption grew
- Development faltered

↓

Draft

In a few countries things have indeed worked out more or less as technocrats expected, but in many countries outcomes were very different. Governments embarked on fanciful schemes. Private investors, lacking confidence in public policies or in the steadfastness of leaders, held back. Powerful rulers acted arbitrarily. Corruption became endemic. Development faltered, and poverty endured.

Topic Government getting bigger

↓

Point Over the last century the size and scope of government have expanded enormously, particularly in the industrial countries.

↓

Support

• Pre–World War II expansion answer to heavy toll taken by Depression
• Postwar confidence caused people to ask for even more
• Industrial countries expanded welfare states
• Developing countries embraced state-dominated development plans
• Size and reach of government ballooned
• Rough statistic on state spending
• Shift from quantitative to qualitative

↓

Draft

Over the last century the size and scope of government have expanded enormously, particularly in the industrial countries. The pre–World War II expansion was driven by, among other factors, the need to address the heavy toll on economic and social systems brought on by the Great Depression. The postwar confidence in government bred demands for it to do more. Industrial economies expanded the welfare state, and much of the developing world embraced state-dominated development strategies. The result was a tremendous expansion in the size and reach of government worldwide. State spending now constitutes almost half of total income in the established industrial countries, and around a quarter in developing countries. But this very increase in the state's influence has also shifted the emphasis from the quantitative to the qualitative.

Topic Clamor for more effective governance

Point The clamor for greater government effectiveness has reached crisis proportions in many developing countries where the state has failed to deliver even such fundamental public goods as property rights, roads, and basic health and education.

Support

• Poor services and people won't pay taxes
• Example in Soviet Union, Eastern Europe
• Collapse of central planning has other problems
• Citizens deprived of basic public goods
• In some places the state crumbles entirely

↓

Draft

The clamor for greater government effectiveness has reached crisis proportions in many developing countries where the state has failed to deliver even such fundamental public goods as property rights, roads, and basic health and education. There a vicious circle has taken hold: people and businesses respond to deteriorating public services by avoiding taxation, which leads to further deterioration in services. In the former Soviet Union and Central and Eastern Europe it was the state's long-term failure to deliver on its promises that led, finally, to its overthrow. But the collapse of central planning has created problems of its own. In the resulting vacuum, citizens are sometimes deprived of basic public goods such as law and order. At the limit, as in Afghanistan, Liberia, and Somalia, the state has sometimes crumbled entirely, leaving individuals and international agencies trying desperately to pick up the pieces.

From the Rockefeller Foundation's report *Into the Working World*

Topic Findings of possible gains

Point New findings from a Rockefeller Foundation study spotlight the possible gains from fully integrated programs of education and employment.

Support

- Findings useful to people working under the Family Support Act
- Focuses on relating basic skills to particular job
- Support for everyday services like child care

Draft

New findings from a Rockefeller Foundation study spotlight the possible gains from fully integrated programs of education and employment. The findings demand the attention of those developing programs of basic education and employment under the Family Support Act. The integrated model focuses employment training on a specific job, relates basic skills training to that job, and tries to meet the precise needs of the local labor market. The model also pulls together support services for handling such everyday problems as child care.

Topic   One site with good results

↓

Point   One of the four sites tested in the Minority Female Single Parent experiment—San Jose's Center for Employment Training—used (indeed, developed) this design with remarkable results.

↓

Support

• Integrated program yielded better jobs and higher wages
• Statistics
• Program worked well for low-income single mothers
• More efficient than traditional programs

↓

Draft

One of the four sites tested in the Minority Female Single Parent experiment—San Jose's Center for Employment Training—used (indeed, developed) this design with remarkable results. When compared with other programs using more traditional designs, the integrated program yielded better jobs and higher wages for a higher proportion of participants. It led to a 27 percent increase in employment and 47 percent higher pay. The integrated program worked well for one of the most difficult groups to get into the work force — low-income single mothers. Moreover, it produced large increases in employment for an amount comparable to what traditional programs spend for similarly disadvantaged enrollees.

Topic In-depth training for a job

Point The integrated model provides in-depth training in the skills required for a specific job

↓

Support

- Other programs fall short for those with substantial disadvantages
- More extensive skills training helps disadvantaged obtain jobs

↓

Draft

The integrated model provides in-depth training in the skills required for a specific job. Less-intensive job-search and work-orientation programs help some people find work, but such programs offer little hope to those with substantial disadvantages, such as low-income single mothers. By contrast, more extensive skills training — in, say, word processing or metalworking — can help disadvantaged trainees obtain good jobs.

Topic   The program placed heavy emphasis on work habits.

↓

Point   Acquiring job skills is only half the training.

↓

Support

- Other half of training focuses on developing life skills
- Develop workers ready to pick up more skills
- Punctuality and attendance

↓

Draft

Acquiring job skills is only half the training. The other half focuses on the development of life skills, self-esteem, and a work ethic. The goal is not merely to produce a skilled word processor or machine tool operator. It is to develop a worker who is punctual, efficient, cooperative, and ready to pick up more skills. The integrated model stresses punctuality and attendance to impart the rhythm of industry. Trainees punch in — not at 8:00 am, but at 7:55 so that they can be at their station by 8:00.

Topic   Plugged into industry

↓

Point   Another key feature of the integrated model is to have the education and employment program plugged directly into the requirements of industry — and to have industry plugged into the development of the program.

↓

Support

- Program developers work with industry personnel to develop curricula
- Training phased out when no demand, added when new demands appear
- Instructors drawn from industry
- Treats training as a business

Draft

Another key feature of the integrated model is to have the education and employment program plugged directly into the requirements of industry—and to have industry plugged into the development of the program. Program developers work closely with production supervisors, personnel managers, and equal opportunity officers to find precisely the skills required and to develop curricula that meet those requirements. When the demand and wages for a skill fall, it is phased out of the skill offerings. When new opportunities appear, they are added. Just as important, technical instructors are drawn from industry. With many years of experience, they know what is needed on the job—the knowledge, skills, and traits needed for success. The integrated approach thus treats training as a business, with the program tailored to community needs, changing market conditions, and the trainee's future work site.

Topic Wraparound support services

↓

Point   Low-income people frequently have big problems and
unstable lives, and sorting out day-to-day affairs can
conflict with training, so support services are provided
in the integrated model.

Support

- Continuing support
- Easy access
- Child care
- Avoid fragmenting trainees' days

Draft

Low-income people frequently have big problems and unstable lives, and sorting out day-to-day affairs can conflict with
training. To avoid such conflict, the integrated model provides
continuing support for the individual. It bolsters the training by
providing easy access to support services that can systematically resolve everyday problems. And for low-income mothers,
the integrated model provides essential child care — at the
training site or at a nearby child care center. The goal is to
avoid fragmenting trainees' days by bouncing them from one
agency to another. Instead, the integrated model tries to provide one-stop continuity for all the support services a person
needs.

SOURCES

Benton Foundation, *The Learning Connection: Schools in the Information Age* (Washington D.C.: Benton Foundation, 1997), pp. ii–iii.

"Geo-political Earthquake," *The Economist* 335, no. 7917 (3 June 1995): 45.

Paul Krugman, "The CPI and the Rat Race," *Slate* (slate.com), 21 December 1996.

The Rockefeller Foundation, *Into the Working World* (New York: The Rockefeller Foundation, 1990), pp. 2–12.

The Survival of the Fittest," *The Economist* 337, no. 7937 (21 October 1995): 92.

UNDP (United Nations Development Programme), *Human Development Report 1995* (New York: Oxford University Press, 1995), pp. 1–29.

UNDP–World Bank, *Water and Sanitation Program Annual Report, July 1994–June 1995* (Washington, D.C.: World Bank, 1996), pp. 64–65.

"Unjammed," *The Economist* 347, no. 8069 (23 May 1998): 74.

U.S. Department of Commerce, Economics and Statistics Administration, Bureau of the Census, *Warmer, Older, More Diverse: State-by-State Population Changes to 2025*, census brief (Washington, D.C.: U.S. Census Bureau, U.S. Department of Commerce, December 1996), CENBR/96-1.

World Bank, *Adjustment in Africa: Reforms, Results, and the Road Ahead* (New York: Oxford University Press, 1994) pp. v–vi.

World Bank, *Claiming the Future: Choosing Prosperity in the Middle East and North Africa* (Washington, D.C.: World Bank, 1995), pp. 1–13.

World Bank, *World Development Report 1997* (New York: Oxford University Press, 1997), pp. v–15.